FIMBUL-WINTER

Also by Debra Allbery:

Walking Distance

FIMBUL-WINTER

Debra Allbery

Four Way Books
Tribeca

Please direct all inquiries to:
Editorial Office
Four Way Books
POB 535, Village Station
New York, NY 10014
www.fourwaybooks.com

Library of Congress Cataloging-in-Publication Data

Allbery, Debra, 1957-
  Fimbul-Winter / Debra Allbery.
     p. cm.
  ISBN 978-1-935536-04-8 (pbk. : alk. paper)
  I. Title.
  PS3551.L377F56 2010
  811'.54--dc22

                           2010001644

This book is manufactured in the United States of America
and printed on acid-free paper.

Four Way Books is a not-for-profit literary press. We are grateful for the assistance
we receive from individual donors, public arts agencies, and private foundations.

This publication is made possible with public funds from the
New York State Council on the Arts, a state agency.

Distributed by University Press of New England
One Court Street, Lebanon, NH 03766

[clmp]   We are a proud member of the Council of Literary Magazines and Presses.

for Matthew and Wyatt

for Mary

So everything is necessary. Every least thing. This is the hard lesson. Nothing can be dispensed with. Nothing despised. Because the seams are hid from us, you see. The joinery. The way in which the world is made . . . .

Cormac McCarthy

To forgo something, that also has its fragrance and its power.

Robert Walser

CONTENTS

Asunder

CHEQUAMEGON

I know how not
to tell this. A dented can
held freezing water from the lake.
It was like washing our hands and faces with fire.
Think of sterno scent, of
coffee grounds. In the van,
upholstery peeling off the seats.

We stopped somewhere
for tools and groceries.
Walked into a reservation bar
to ask directions. The darkling rusted
swivel of that place.
Its heavy door.

It was April, ice
still edging everything.
Each breath a drink
of well water laced with tin.

We climbed a fire tower,
wind splintering off its metal grids.
Later we stood on a pier
as narrow as a gangplank,
the blue-black wince of the lake
glinting all around us.

In the woods I let him say
his words. They sounded
like leaves, years
and years of leaves.

But this is where
I get lost every time.
The bare trees. What I didn't do.
His ghost laugh loose above me,
red strip of cellophane snagged
in the grass. When we walked back
half of the trees we passed
were marked for cutting, yellow bull's-eyes,
a slapped splash of suns. I followed him
through the birches. I disappeared.

CURES AND MAXIMS

after the Old English

Write this on a housel dish
in the beginning was the word in heaven's might
and high hall Then wash the writing
into water fetched against a stream

> *frost must freeze and fire burn*
> *ice must form a bridge*

For wooden heart add bonewort lupin
and everfern to holy water and circle
the vessel three times   Drink the draught
when day and night divide

> *a coward's heart has no room for courage*

Sing this incantation into a wound
twelve times under linden under light-shield
grow smaller not greater Smear the salve
thrice in the sign of the cross

> *the solemn path of the dead is the longest secret*

Before a journey put artemisia in your shoe
and pray *ne lassus sum in via*
thaes oferede   thisses swa maeg
don't let me be weary along the way

> *that passed   and so may this*

Cyclone Cellar

The dream looks like a drawing.
An etching. Photogravure.
Except I hear his voice—
he's talking again about
bad timing, blaming himself.

How small he's become, turned toward
the wall in his basement corner.
He's in an exposed foundation,
as if a tornado had lifted the house.
I sit above, on the sand.

I'm hemming a fine white square
of linen while he explains
and explains. How different
his story is from mine.
He's the size of my thumb.

The less I listen the more
his lines blunt and roughen
into pencil. Grisaille, a dissolve
into chaff and dust, into
that old chant, *one, one—*

CHRONIC TOWN

If I listen to that year now,
it's a traffic song in winter, the gray hum
of the skyway arched over eight broad lanes,
the metal rattle of the freight lift in my building.
I lived in a converted nurses' dormitory—
pocked cinderblocks, mattress on the floor.
Green floors and walls, the air itself washed through
with the faint sweet green of convalescence.
Whole families lived in some of the rooms—
taut pierces of Chinese or Korean through the walls.

I'd found work in scholarly texts and reference
in the basement of a college bookstore.
We had a dying customer, George,
who always asked for me. His mother
would wheel him behind the counter,
and I'd bend down low to take his order—
mathematics, linguistics, Russian novels.
Two or three words could ride out on each breath,
but barely formed, almost inaudible.
It took all my concentration to hear him.
When he'd leave, my throat would be tense from trying
to grasp and shape each phantom word.
From trying to speak for him.
The shallow wind of his voice would tremble
through me all day, medicinal, floral.

Nothing to go home to,
I'd walk that icebound city into dark,
the threadbare shadows of the thin days
wrapped tight around me.

And would lose myself in the littered streets
until the cold pressed through and drove me inside.
In the library the homeless slept upright
at long tables, gripping their open books.
I'd sit there just listening to the slow scuff
of my own heart, the useless letter
it kept rewriting. In my pocket a scrap
of paper, pressed into my palm weeks before
by a deaf customer whose fierce signs I couldn't read.
An intricate glyph, a treble clef in barbed wire—
the buried title of every book he needed.

FIMBUL-WINTER

*First will come the winter called Fimbulvetr. Snow will drive from
all quarters, there will be hard frosts and biting winds, the sun will be
no use. There will be three such winters with no summer between.*
from The Prose Edda of Snorri Sturluson

1.   BETWEEN LAKES

To wake from a corridor
into a corridor. Five a.m., crossing
the chilled tiles to the stove,
hands hovering over spirals
of heat. Then the water-note
of the kettle.

Something land's-end about the place,
something uncharted: a narrow isthmus
between single-syllable lakes.
The camouflaged silence
of those early autumn mornings—
hunters in their blinds, fishermen,
the hushed wakes of their boats.

If there had been a way out,
a sign that wasn't a barricade.
Sundays, the short isthmus
between work-weeks—a walk
along either shore; the thin,
complacent reach of the waves.
Piers stacked in sections
on the leaf-strewn beaches—
half-bridges drawn in before
each lake closes its eye.

At night the rising winds parting sleep
like marsh grasses, a low rustling,
a held breath. Then the high tangle
of the first flakes caged in the branches.

2.   WORK

December dawn cloaked in the numb dark of midnight,
subzero air sifting into the lungs like snow,
snow ticking like glassy sand. Its soft scour,
its swift wing sweeping each footprint.

Each morning he's always a hundred yards ahead,
his slumped weight rising out of a car's idling exhaust,
rolled cap and rumpled coat, black against the snowlight.
Then the car's cough and sputter as it approaches

and churns past—driverless, scraped frost and fumes,
its back left window rolled down. The snapping snouts
of three dogs barely visible, blunt barks
freezing just before they reach the ground.

3.   NEW YEAR

Not the braced air of the lean winters,
the grayed yellow wash of afternoon;
not the whistle-down of the crossroads,
its emptiness boxing the ears.

Not the stiff ruff of the fields, their reedy bones
birdless, the snag and trundle of leaves.
The red hummed shudder of a stop sign
while mute hills carve the horizon.

Not the press of the blank sky.
Not the sky with every door closed.

4.   OF SNOW

> The snow that falleth where it is tolerably cold
> and rainy withal falls like unto small roses or needles.
>
> F. Martens, *Voyage to Spitzbergen*

That night a white border between the inhabited and the uninhabited.
January, three years before, almost forty below.

The snow-choked streets gone dark from the icestorm,
glazed branches shriven and littering the brittle drifts.

> When the cold weather doth remit, the snow falleth like stars,
> with many points, like the leaves of ferne.

The night still, except for a distant high shearing
of the heavens, a shook-foil chafing of cold against dark.

Brief drift of fierce stars, then the clouds' pale occlusion.
My own hands and feet losing their edges—

frostbite limning an old scar on my index finger,
settling into a small patch in my palm.

Ahead, white giving way to white, the trees receding
and then vanishing, every means of reckoning gone.

> *When it is very cold but not windy withal, the snow falleth like stars*
> *in a cluster because the wind cannot blow them asunder.*

5.   ASUNDER

Twelve miles north the road ended,
split sharp into east and west. Ahead, just the frozen wreckage
of another lake, broken and buckled in the land's tight embrace—
jutted plates of ice like shattered tablets,
smashed prows caught in gray-pearl cubist waves.

The wind strafing its northern bluster across it.
Splinter song, old saga.
Quick scythe through the lungs.

Stops here—the March sky stripped bare.
At the end of the pier, the slack flag rope slapping
against its frosted pole like a dead bell.

I used to think that I needed a hard life,
that every surface I touched ought to be rough.
I wanted the air to be sharp and thin.
A field without footprint or signature.

Now the ice-rutted road stretches south like half an idea,
red snow fence trailing off in mid-sentence.

The wind combs the matted grasses in the fields on either side,
hums through the bent ribs of a hayrake.
Then the crow lifts a black wingbeat—a half brushstroke,
        a blinked eyelash
against the sky's white reach.

IMAGINARY

THE ASSIGNATION

London Monday on the tube to Hampstead,
its lurch and jar, its tunnel vision.
You wait without watching in the posh sunlight.
Our walk is only want. The polished
dark of an eighteenth-century pub,
the laden bees in Keats's lavender.
Inside his house we lift velvet panels
to see glass-cased letters, pale locks
of hair. His still perfect bed behind
its wall of glass, airless, pressuring
don't touch, don't touch. In the car
at the station, the press and wild theft
of a kiss, then bereft, then gone
to Glasgow. Gone to Teneriffe.

CONSTELLATION

*Because he desperately needed an imaginary eye to follow his life
he would occasionally write her long letters.*
Milan Kundera

Dear C—
      At dawn I drove to Wilder Dam,
parked in that rutted lot that faces the river.
The Connecticut looked so glassy, still, so *liquid*—
reflections of trees and houses lay solid, slick,
a wet floor that might be carefully walked across.
A bandy-legged old man stood casting his line
toward his double, his bloodhound asleep beside him.
The breezes still carried night from beneath the trees,
edges of the opal sky beginning to darken
and concentrate toward the midday heat.
I just sat there in the still shimmer of things,
my car pointed dumbly toward the water,
the way people do at the shore. Then drove away.

Back here, a lute and birdsong Sunday,
blessed. I paced in the solitude,
wasting it in listening for it to end.
Then sat outside on my upstairs steps
with coffee, books. Even the mornings are heavy
with late summer heat, the undone,
indolence—My head's the buzz and drone
of trundling insects and thickening light,
the warm scent of my own skin in this sun.
But you remember how brief summer is here—
a few pages, a camera flash of light and heat,
a blurred green photograph lost in a desk drawer.

Two years now since you left for your far east,
your handwriting slowly becoming your face
and voice. Then your script, too, surfacing
as if from a dream. Sometimes I still address
envelopes to you, I even stamp them,
stand them empty, weightless, on my desk.
But the words they might hold stay inside me now,
small lamps that flare and burn out underground.

Walking, I heard these this week:
He has a good sense of human.
And: *It was an act of luck.*
And two students crossing the street, one saying
In my dreams, at the moment of truth—
I lost the rest. But he said it with such fervor,
it was as if I'd never heard the phrase before.

In my dreams your illumined letters fly
sealed, translucent, high above the ocean,
gliding and circling down like white birds
destined for my hands. The sea bears me out
to meet them—as if I were in a boat,
but there's no boat.

What can I write you of this place
that you don't already know and carry?
The woods are still lit with the slender
trunks of birches, the pines still sweep
the same note through the forest.

This afternoon thunderheads sailed in,
a brief rain fell through the broken light.
And now this evening—the sky's soft-spoken iris,
the quiet blue of sleep between two dreams.

Last night I dreamed myself putting on
a winter coat. It resembled my coat closely,
but then I understood that it was yours.
The coat was so heavy and long, it held me still.
Then you stepped out from the shadows, pleased.
You wanted me to be surprised, but I wasn't
and didn't feel like pretending that I was.
"Aren't you surprised to see me?" you asked.
I slipped off the coat and held it out to you.

Today on the interstate I saw a man
lying on his back in front of his parked car
there on the graveled shoulder of the highway.
He had his arms folded behind his head—
he was just staring up at the hillside, at the sky.
All the speeding, wary cars were switching lanes
as they passed him. He lay there as if he
were in some meadow or park, his head only
inches away from his front tire—just below
his license plate that said BEGIN.

Where you are it's early tomorrow morning.
I see you stepping from the curb and disappearing
into the anarchic traffic of a Taipei
I've constructed only from your scholar's prose,
pressed over foreign noise and the treble hum

of what you will not say. I know you need
to be able to picture me here, a friend
tending to your memory in a remembered place.
What do you do with them now, the sentences
you don't send me?

These days, when I think back to when you were here,
to how you would point out landscapes and constellations
so the sight and memory of them could be shared, doubled,
I think it was also to keep me looking away,
to keep my gaze outside your uncertain eyes.
Packing today, I found the dried iris petals,
the flowers you surprised me with one Sunday morning.
I'd saved them, kept them in a covered porcelain bowl,
then forgot them in a drawer. Their curled blue questions.

I drove down the river road again
at twilight, the last petals of sunset
scattered on the water—and opposite, the moon
was already above the hills—weirdly full,
improbable—it looked too close, too heavy.
I pulled over and got out, sat there
studying the sky. You'd stopped the car near there
once, one December night, to point out Orion.
And spoke of your long affinity with that hunter—
But now when I try to piece the words together
it sounds like one of our transoceanic calls—
snips of sound cut out, split-second delays
making our words rift and overlap, your voice
muddied as if underwater.

I know that Orion means *foot-turning wanderer*.
That Rigel, the brilliant star marking his left foot,
is actually two stars revolving around each other.

In your last letter you described a Poste Restante
in Nepal, the grandeur of its disrepair,
a purgatory of correspondence.
Dim light forcing through a few high windows
and the silted air, the fluttered shadows
of pigeons in the rafters. And far below,
all the brittle paper whispers—
you thumbing through long wooden trays
of envelopes, looking for your name.

FIRELANDS

Of my childhood I remember almost nothing.
Backyards rubbed raw by hard play and chained dogs.
The sepia velour of our Pontiac, flat blur
of cornfields and refineries. In summer,
propping up my bedroom window with a scrap
of plywood, the heft and heavy rattle of warped glass.
Cut grass. The slams and sighs of factories.

One August night when I was twelve, I woke
to the silent swoop of alarm, my bedroom bright
from a fire at the Silver Fleece, a closed cannery
two blocks away. The abandon of those flames,
shooting out of nowhere, smoke scouring the stars.
I watched it. I let everybody sleep.

A mine fire burned beneath my mother's
southern Ohio hometown for a hundred years.
My grandfather could remember water boiling
in their wells, baked potatoes in the gardens.
Cut a gash in a hillside and smoke would rise.
Now that country is all ghost towns, the strikers' rage
smoldering finally into depletion and collapse,
sink holes opening behind the abandoned schools.

Firelands, the signs said around my own small town—
banks, a real estate office. But that was history's ash,
the British burning the Western Reserve. The world is on fire,
wrote Sherwood Anderson, who grew up four streets over
from my house. The sidewalks and feed store are burning up,
decay you see is always going on.

We knew that there, the pocked pith of railroad ties
crumbling into dust, the hitching rails
no one had bothered to remove leaving smears of rust
on our hands and clothes. There was nothing
in that still town to be afraid of, but night after night
I wrenched myself from dreams I refused to repeat.
My mother would sit beside me in the dark,
consigning every worry back underground.

SHORT STORY

A stupid joke, nerves talking: that men like
younger women because their stories are shorter.
Iowa, October, twenty years ago now,

how I leaned into her listening, told her the years
I'd locked away. Oslo, Brussels, Canada,
the war at home. Her questions weaving through,

fingers in my belt loops, while back at the house
my wife was drawing the curtains, turning off
the lights. Long nights, in nearby towns,

how we'd lie, afterwards, damp bodies clasped
around each other, trying to be one past,
a single story. I'd wake and watch dawn freeze

around the hard lines of the motel room.
Or at her place, in a boarding house that backed up
to a cornfield. The spare, unwritten expanse

of her life—bare walls, neat stack of journals.
Everything was paper!—even the calm
of her sleeping face. I'd run my hands over

the spines of her books and shiver; in my dreams
I left fingerprints, muddy tracks. But guilt
sharpens a man's edges, and when the time came

I just drove away for good without a word.
Now, miles and years away, not much remains.
Divorce, remarriage—a woman who, thank God,

doesn't listen, leaves me alone. I walk out,
follow the road until the pavement stops,
then make my pathless hike into the hills.

Life falls away. Her scent, her circling arms,
the loose braid of our night voices.
Whatever's left I leave for her to tell.

IMAGINARY

Kalispell last night, a highway payphone, he dialed her number.
Recognition slanting her voice like the trace of an accent
she had tried to lose. *Who is this?* she had repeated into the static,
then colder, quieter, *Who is this.* And him not answering,

just trying her name, the small shape of it, saying *Would you please
talk to me*, ice-rough rain slicing through, until, after a few long minutes,
she hung up. He's sure she'll think but never believe it was him,
not after all these years, and the black cloth of distance, the weather's erasures.

THE BORDERS

Near the Canongate, the russet drift of centuries
of blood still ghosting from the cobblestones.
Damp air abraded with American laughter,
its swaggered pitch and swath. Took refuge
in the dim settled silence of a bookshop,
frayed bindings and familiar foxed must.
Read for an hour by the folly, and then,
midday, climbed Arthur's Seat alongside
some Glaswegians, their accent impenetrable
but rilling, warm-timbred. Edwin Muir
we had in common, lost Edens, that rowing
forever from the stony known. *There is a road
that turning always / Cuts off the country
of Again.* From the top, the blackened prow
of the castle, the Firth of Forth, grassy seas
without building or boundary. Country
of Erstwhile, of Meanwhile, of Still.

AFTER

After the Auction of My Grandmother's Farm

My father has secretly taken up whittling.
He's hollowed a piece of pine into a box
and inside I find tiny, unfinished toys—
lopsided tops, and snowflakes small as jacks,
with missing points. The wood is so soft
I could press my thumbprint into it.

A long winter is coming. I can tell
by the way the hogs huddle silent in their pen.
I stand on a bowed, gray slat of their fence
and they don't even look, their curved white backs
lined up like dim eggs in the failing light.

In my grandmother's house an artist
stands at his easel. His canvases are everywhere—
all larger than himself, and all the same:
paintings of a doorframe open to darkness.
The room is only doors. I walk out

past the swaybacked barn, past the mailbox.
A moonlit dog trots toward us—silvered dust,
his eyes the color of water. And then a man
appears, my grandfather. I know him from dreams,
his smile, his slouch hat. He opens the pasture gate.
The dog bounds ahead of us, into the posted woods.

How to Explain Pictures to a Dead Hare

Joseph Beuys at Galerie Schmela
Dusseldorf, 1965

1.
The woman walks a bramble
of quiet fright, her tenses
frayed. Any pencil touch
not light enough.

*

No Leda. Only fierce
ur-flight, a thrum, a wish of wings—
Only dashed speech, then
upsweep, the god's ascent.

*

How the hand knows
its own name and writes it
blind. Then something washes
over the word.

*

Golgotha. Or else Kleve,
after the war. A dream I had once—
ochre shouts, a *braunkreuz*
thrown through the thick breath of shadows.

2.
True is this event during the war:
When the Tartars found me after the plane crash
they wrapped me in felt and fur,
they salved my wounds with lard.

Sometimes these things are looked at
in a false way, these accidents, damages
to my body, these wounds. They are not secret
affinities. They are not only mine.

3.
Gold leaf pressed into
his face's harrowed gaunt.
Soft slack of the animal
in his arms, his stroke piano—

4.
This is a map of the ruined city,
a shaft of lightning in the pine.
Blood sky, foxed twilight,
the trees sound like waiting.

*

This is a word thought
but not spoken. This is how
it listens to itself—its slow whorl
of force, the sure press of its thumbprint.

Frame

Sunday afternoon in the two-hearted woods,
clouded brow of the upper Midwest.

Juncoes flick on the frozen sill, then tack
to the shelter of the woodpile. From my window
I can see the window of my dark classroom.
My own narrow hard-packed path in the snow,
meridian between the workday's two poles.

In my lap the glossed weight of a book on Courbet.
The Fringe of the Forest, Trees in the Snow—
fathomless blacks, their surged strokes
filling the room like dusk. The tidy silence
of these days, gleaming floorboards.
Everything staying just as I leave it.

The sky hovers close here, its gray blanket
flying just over our heads, fastened down
a few miles to the north. It pulls away
along the horizon at sunset, the light there
flaring riotous, or else blind mute yellow.
A raised window, a breathing space.

Paysages du neige. This morning
I drove twelve miles just to mail a letter
to a love long since lost, the words lying
cool and cloistered in their envelope, my hand
warming a postscript into its blank.
I drive out every day over the frost heaves

and ruts to see something other than
this framed grotto of pine—the straw patience
of sawgrass, white scraps of waterbirds
in the marsh. Gray lake humming into gray sky.
This morning, a tight S-band of horses, stilled

beneath a mantle of fog. Like *Burial at Ornans*,
the mourners pressed between the firmaments.

CLEAR MIRROR LAMENT

after Meng Hao-jan

narcissus in bloom behind rimed glass
green shoots bow low to their forced bulbs

winter pond a bright gibbous moon
geese cut their accents above the pines

we walked this path under summer stars
mock-orange petals scattered like snowflakes

how could farewell go so long and so far
still each breath blooms white

OFFICE

the way the doors' double intake has that
    little extra suck of air the pull of vacuum
and wake a whisked scrape of dry leaves
    spiraling then scattering their last rasp behind her
as the doors seal and her eyes dim under the dark
    hood of fluorescence the slow hummed heavy
gravity of commerce its narrow hall the color
    of dolor of compliance she sits and presses
power buttons on and on their wheezed whirring
    like a scour a spun erasing inside her those
loosed leaves somewhere still scribbling something
    she used to know how to read

After Vermeer

1.   *Woman Holding a Balance*

Still the map surprises. What's near now,
what's newly distant. Nothing finds me here,
no letters, none of my usual dreams.
Overcast warps through the leaded glass
of our bedroom window, the morning light
presses into a porcelain cup on the sill.

My husband's eyes move beneath his lids
as if he were reading. Last night I dreamed him
standing on a ladder in the rain,
trying to clear out some leaf-clogged gutters,
while below his father muttered advice to the ground,
hand raised in an irritated benediction.
Then my husband lifted a small doll by one heel
from the eaves, brackish water draining
from its joints, its open eyes.

Is it ever how we've imagined? I wake up lost,
then watch the dawn's dim shadows take on weight,
and the room becomes every other room
where I have lived, the window any window
I've looked through. Outside, the threadbare browns
of early winter, the frost-stunned grass,
tiny tremors of wind. The inanimate
take on life for a moment, then are revealed:
a scrap of writing paper, a discarded glove.
Sympathy—the word hung in a glass charm
from a gold bracelet I wore when I was a girl.

What is mine now is only what I keep to myself—
a clutch of secrets like the tightened mass
of another life inside me, a phantom fullness
I can never name, a quickening.
And yet in marriage what isn't given away?
Without looking back, I can see his sleep,
the way the worn light finds him, darkness
folding itself away like a heavy drape.
And in his dream, perhaps, is my own hand,
resting on the clean edge of a table.

2.   *Girl Asleep at a Table*

The inside-out of waking, my blue-lipped dream
just breaking up: a banquet, your late entrance.
The guests' eyes lifting,
turning a question toward me.

I saw your shadow leaning in the doorway.
You bowed to me with an absurd flourish.
Something wrong with your smile,
the shape of your teeth.

This morning in Greyfriars churchyard
an old man limped toward me, apologizing
for his outstretched hand.
See my head keeps bleeding, he said,

and my hands. My hands are broke.
He turned them over and over
as if in wonder, his wet-dog smell
roping itself around me, and I backed away—

not frightened of him, just angry
at my own wants. I mumbled sorry
and hurried out the gates. His scent
ghosting around me, rising from the cobbles.

I lost myself in the market,
all the damp vendors and their cold flowers.
A blind man took my wrist—*You're happy today—*
and I couldn't answer, held by his unfixed stare.

Home now, by this fire, I can't get warm.
Still, it's enough to be inside, to just sit still
here at this table and lean my head
against my hand, feel how it feels to lean,

to rest against something. As sleep hovers,
touches, enters. *Always, always,* it murmurs,
a breath from your grave. You used to palm
the word, play shell games with it.

Now, love, it's no mystery. Close your eyes.
The room is the same inside me, then falls away.
Crosshatch, spindle. Just blind lost light.
Only my own hands holding me up.

3.   *Woman in Blue Reading a Letter*

The calm passes overhead like cloud shadow,
darkens the eggshell walls.

Outside, spring's rainlight,
the pale new medallions of leaves

caught in the wind's strumming.
The closer I come to my confinement,

the more I shawl my past around me.
Three months now he's sailed. I pull

old boxes down, finger trinkets from my childhood—
a tiny pin shaped like a beetle, a twig

in a sealed jar once filled with river water.
Its green still dusts the glass.

And in a box of letters, one stamped
and addressed to my grandmother, labeled

To be opened when I am grown up.
How strange to deliver this to myself

twenty-five years later—how strange
to me, my own young hand. The letters

curled back into themselves,
small fists, ferns still furled.

I write of a flood. Simple descriptions:
The streets are like rivers. Our water isn't safe.

I can't remember why I chose to save this.
I remember the flood. Seeing my father out in it.

And the smell—the waterlogged bricks
in our cellar, crumbling to the touch.

Sometimes I dream our child is buried alive.
I know where she is, but still I choose to ignore her

and she's furious, down in her little pocket of earth,
angry enough to claw her own escape.

Who would I tell this to. If I stand still enough
the room's silence and mine create a sound

between them, the round note
of a cello, a generated third.

SONG

RIDDLE

the wave, over the wave . . . water become bone
—*The Exeter Book, riddle 68*

The spring that cleaved to winter
The river that sealed itself

The promise with its pulled thread
The wind that sang through the weave

The words in their long cloaks
Wave over wave

The cry in its glass box
Water become bone

Cloud breath closing
Voice swallowing voice

Say truly what my name is
Say what I am called

No Tutor But the North

After the fifth storm the ridges of plowed snow
rose so high on either side of the narrow street

those who lived there had to sculpt their parking spaces,
carve them out like little caves, arced alcoves.

Each morning when people left for work they'd save
their spaces with old dinette chairs, rusted chrome

and vinyl relics pulled from basements, attics.
Those desultory chairs made the daytime street

look like it had given up waiting for a parade.
Or sometimes I thought they looked like unnamed

gravestones, blank and unkempt sentries, but
solemn, dignified in their simple duty.

*

Jim Dine's photographs of crows and owls are sheened
shadows on the heart, presentiment,
oracle—sometimes posed indoors

with old toys and torn chairs, or in an outdoors that's dream-lit,
uncanny. *My birds were my friends, they were me,*
he writes. *They were my library.*

*

Ice-skinned footprints flinting under my step.
Blink of snowflakes on my sleeve.

Bare trees like forked tongues,
or pokers stirring the clouded ashes of a cold fire.

*

the dark caul of December

the sudden, awful splay of wings on my windshield,
not once but twice, the forced print

of that omen, the flayed flight,
then nothing. Tu Fu's

fluttering, fluttering—where is my likeness?

—the blood's yes, then no

*

Dine writes, *Winter is the time I learn most things, I'm indoors
and within myself.* And then: *I mainly rode my bicycle.
Skidding all over the ice I rode my bicycle continuously.*

In some of the crow photos is Dine's own hand, open
or cupped. *This is the dream part, this is the me part.*
He names the crow Jimmy, calls the dream *North.*

*

This is the me part: a hand opened,
then closed. Empty cup, little ice cave.
What persists but has no body:
the slant-rhyme of our lives. Engraved,
this infant memory, *a gull between heaven
and earth.*

CLINIC

In the center of the waiting room there's a talk show—
jabbed speech, a hazard of accents, the dull mirror
of audience smiling up at themselves.

And around the television a thick, blurred orbit
of inattention, a scattered askance. Women staring,
then glancing down at magazines, their worn pages

gone soft as cloth. The TV dissolving to snow.
Its little sparks, its busy horizon. Quarks from the beginning
of beginnings still blinking their first messages.

The Wakeful Bird Sings Darkling

Our tiny plot of a cottage was cloaked
in pine at the graveled close of a sidestreet,
undercover, overgrown, September sprawl
of raspberries lost again to the blackbirds.
The sun could never find its way
to our windows; the walls were thick
as a bunker's, stolid, stone and stone
and stone. The baby sick again,
as he was for most of his first year,
his fevered sleep fast in my arms. That morning
the phone rang, my husband out in his real life,
calling just from work, but the line staticked
and broken as if from a great distance,
saying to turn on the TV. And so I did,
just in time to see the first tower fall, then
the slant silent drift of a plane, the little bloom
of fire, the smoke's ashen pillar and pall.
The baby's glittering eyes fixed only on me.

We went out back then, sat on the crumbling stoop,
where just three months before our yellow cat,
Rover, had dragged himself after a stroke.
Back left paw trailing, curled under, his pupils
faint pinpoints of terror. *Lamb of God,*
my husband would call it when he draped him,
purring, like a stole over his shoulders,
but his last day he wouldn't even let me touch him,
hissing from the closet's dark. The vet
had to come for him, wearing falconer's gloves.

That September morning's iris of sky just as fierce,
stripped and raw, too close; I shielded the baby
with my shadow. Then the quiet was ripped
by the ratchet of a kingfisher plummeting
from the power lines into the dark mirror
of our pond. The whole world a dim window
I couldn't see through, my focus only this
instant, this infant listless and flushed
in my arms. I whispered the rapid count
of his breaths per minute, trying
to determine the line between self-reliance
and when we'd need help.

ALL WE NEED

Purblind twilight, Michigan's mum
in snow blankets and bird cloaks—
grackles blackleafing two oaks and a locust,
then taking flight in a swarm. The tree trunks
straighten into single digits.

House on the hill behind them,
its arched windows lit. So many years
I woke into cold, single rooms, and now.
Now we have all we need.

Even plenty has its ache. Two winters ago,
another life inside me, I walked
stubbornly centerless on the ice.
Now that child wakes to the dark dawn,
looks out at the dim sparrows

scavenging in the snow. *No,*
he calls it, *no, no.*

The Woman's Lament

after the Old English

This song of sorrow's journey
is mine alone to sing,
its lines layered and shifting
over the years, but never
weighted more with grief than now.

My beloved's betrayal
was a glanced absence that grew
over time, and in time
I was left to my own course, exiled
and friendless within my own house.
Dawn-sorrow marked the dark valley
of the winter when his false heart
first spoke its name,
my mind and the days briar-caged.
To find that my soul's own
companion had so concealed
himself, as if we had never loved.

So I abide, too, in hiding now,
abandoned, in cave and grove,
my restless heart conjuring
the gray waves that swell
toward his own storm-struck coast.

May his days wear laughter's mask
over a loss that never lessens.

May longing ever be his dwelling,
as it is mine.

Casting Off

Little warrior, buoyant blessing, night falls
        and we cast off again. You curve yourself
            back into your beginnings, cleave

to sleep's shoreline, ride the shallow crests
        of my breath. So many nights,
            those first twilit months of your life,

I would wake frantic between feedings,
        certain you were swallowed in our blankets.
            I'd sit bolt upright, blind, dull hands

desperate to find you. The bed a black sea
        rocking around me, and I the lost one,
            foundering like flotsam. Your father's

back to me, drifting further and further away.
        And then I'd hear your calm measure
            in the crib, I'd see you swaddled.

At your age now, I should leave you storied,
        kissed, and drowsy in your bed, but still
            you say *rock*, and I lift you,

my only anchor, into this chair, and listen as
        our breathing changes keys. The tethered course
            of this ferry, our moored unmooring—

FAULT

Small, she took the shape of the mistake
his shame would not admit. In dreams he crept
as wounded wolf or fox, its grey fur gashed.
Sprung trap, a black blood trail, the dark washed through

with snow. Then dawn would prize his sleep—his wife
of ten years turned away, awake, watching
the first light cloak itself in its widow's weeds.
The precision of her silence, its care and grasp,

her breath a folded wing. How small of her,
he'd think, to make his breach so large.
Her eyes black shades. His stopped hands empty, closed.
Her own fault, this grief. He'd lie there, caught.

THIS IS A SONG

Early that fell-swoop spring, after supper,
my two-year-old son and I would pull on unboxed jackets,
wrinkled as new leaves, and would step outside
for a game of catch. *No hats?* he'd ask, doubtful,
cold being most of what he'd known, and I smiled
like a conspirator, *No hats.* The trees still bent
and dazed with the swiped backhand of winter—
the whole landscape swayed east, battered,
flattened, blanched. *Up high,* he'd command,

and I'd toss the red ball with its glittery specks
into the sky's startled, unaccustomed blue.
Gravity itself thin and unsure, something
to be relearned—I'd zig and zag to catch,
and let it bounce beyond my grasp, or would snag it
from the air, staggering backwards with the effort,
until his own delight would fell him in imitation—
I fall down, oh no, I fall down—the stunted brown grass
holding us a moment with its own slow waking.

I'd gather him up then and take us to the fence,
look down at the two neighbor houses in the valley—
the tattooed couple with their Harleys and pit bulls,
and the kind, close family—mother, father, five-year-old,
taking small turns around their yard on the lawn tractor.
Like the tight little spools of children's rhymes
and songs that unwound themselves within,
back then, behind any moment of quiet.
The little fur father said goodbye one day,
put on his hat and went away
out into his little fur world . . . .

Our own long lane empty, chalky, still.
Night falling fast, as it does early on.
No sullen headlights crawling up the drive.
Just the nascent, breathless weeds, the vertiginous
dissolve of our watch. My son's head pressed
against my heart's hammered falter.

And would carry him inside then to bath and bed
and books, singing *Sleep, sleep, my little fur child,*
out of the windiness, out of the wild,
remembering how, running home in the story,

the child mistook his mother, coming to meet him,
for the dark. Her warm expanse nothing
like the black fields behind my eyes, the shadows
my lullabies dragged. *Where is our laugh?*
my son asked me once. *Where does it live inside us?*

NIGHTINGALE

Once upon a time there was a watch
        that had no face. It kept its time to itself
like a thought or a secret room. No one wanted
        such a watch. They needed Time to have hands
hurrying them through each day's steady vanishings.
        Discarded, lost, the watch found itself tossed
along a narrow park path, its crystal shattered,
        but all its hidden thin-toothed gears still turning.
A boy found it and took it home as a treasure.
        He thought of it as a bird heart, a combination
lock, a music box. Its precise containment
        reminded him of his father's measuring tape—
the long reach and rapid, trim retreat
        as it snapped itself back into its silver shell,
He placed the watch by his bedside and when he woke
        in the night, as he often did, he would sit
in the moonlight and cradle its small stirring. It was
        a mother's song, he decided, both a heartbeat
and a hum, a river with all its words inside it.

RIVER

RUACH

under the parched sky, in the bleached-bone grass.
Amarillo sunset, late August. *Sometimes God
is a nice wind,* my son says, his thin voice
buffeted, t-shirt rippling like a flag.
Black plume rising from the treeless horizon,
range fires ten miles past the wind farms.
The Pentecostal tongues there leaping
gullies and dirt roads, whole fields
going up like tinder, but from here

just another smudged erasure
behind us. He spins clockwise and counter
as we head west in the dense heat
to where our road ends in cattle
and corn stubble, plowed dust spiraling
its brown haze. He shields his eyes,
squints up, *Mrs. M. told us Texas*

is closer to the Lord. I crouch down
beside him to see what he sees.
Tumbleweeds, some of them the size
of a small boy, bounding worn-thorned
and wild as untethered joy across the barren
ocean of grass. Days before they reach
the next fence. *The grass withers,*

says Isaiah, *because the breath
of the Lord blows on it. Surely
the people are grass.* Sun's blood-

shimmer in a blazed wake of sky, the wind's
traveling song whistling its fine grit
in our teeth. We're closer to something here,
and it swallows us whole, wicks us as quick
as sweat. We turn back into the charred blasts,
and it feels like release. Feels like world without end.

River

You want to tell this story
without touching anything.
The glass unsmudged, the great river
still frozen. Or if it was raining then,
the rain falling unbroken.

There are no people in this story,
no one you'd know. It's January,
March, that fine gray suspension
before the thaw. It's a long walk,
that's all, hands deep in the pockets,

rough wind of diesel and prairie,
years go by. You carry a few words
like compasses, that's all, like coins,
bright eye-pennies, their cool weight
precise in the palms.

BRIGHT ABSENTEE

Some Sailor, skirting foreign shores –
Some pale Reporter, from the awful doors
Before the Seal!
      Emily Dickinson

slant season   translated
house

dear Uncle this early spring
morning I imagine

your ample eye   the fathom
of your pen

white curtains describing breezes
from opposite seas

coming to anchor, is the most
that I can do

PIAZZA DI SPAGNA, 1821

During his last days Keats often held a cornelian given to him by
Fanny Brawne. Joseph Severn wrote that the stone seemed
"his only consolation, the only thing left him in this world clearly tangible."

A month from now, the authorities will scrape
the plaster from your walls, will burn your clothes
and books, your bed. The chair in which your friend
now sleeps, his slow breath lighting on your skin

like ice. These final mornings you still hold
the measure of your days like this cornelian,
oval as a bird's egg, in your palm,
the stone that cooled her hand during needlework.

You shift its small round weight. Behind your eyes,
behind your memory's quiet alchemy,
all you have owned or touched already burns.
Awake, asleep, you grasp the last of it—

this warmed stone, the heart's banked coals, the passing
of breath's brief syllable to death's whole note.

LESSON

Charles calls from the veranda,
his wave a hello, a beckon.
August morning, white gold—
a Sunday filter on the lens,
the light pulled into pinch-pleats.

He leads me through empty rooms—
blind blond of floorboards, the windows
bright flags—then out on a balcony
as narrow as a catwalk. Thin music
rising—Bessie Smith singing Dylan:

Don't go mistaking paradise
for that house across the road.
Everywhere the leaves' dumbshow,
green skittle of softshoe. The road below
bonedust, and broad as noon.

EARTHBOUND

As we might rest in the shift of a shadow,
oblique comfort of an angle telling the time—
driving deeper into summer every evening,
the wheatfields making their familiar passage
from pale green to sea gray to tarnished gold.
The west wind's rote hand passing over the grain,
absent touch, and yet the press of that certainty,
year upon year. Same sequence, inevitable

outcome. The road's worn curves crumble,
gray fenceposts tick past. My son's eyes fixed
on flight, *redtail, peregrine.* And mine
on the field's new blank lines, the slow settle
of twilight over the combines' undoing,
their scythed whispers flickering down the rows.

CARPATHIAN FRONTIER

. . . like something thoughtlessly,
Mistakenly erased, the road simply ended.
Larry Levis, "The Widening Spell of the Leaves"

A foreign street, a crooked finger of shops,
dusk falling behind their steep-pitched roofs.
Each window glazed a green-lit yellow
and framing someone at work: a calligrapher pausing
before the brushstroke, a girl bent over lace.
I hold an address folded in my pocket.

What I want is a photograph
of my dead teacher, and I've been told
that a woman on this street can create it.
When I walk in, she sits me down, smiling.
Her hands on my head this way, that.
Then into a darkroom to lift the paper from its bath.

He's sitting alone on a jetty, he's saying
something—one large hand raised slightly
in an indeterminate gesture, open grace
of the fingers tracing some missing word.
Around him a rubble of bleached rocks
and broken concrete—and the jetty is cracked:

a long, widening fissure which will island him
eventually, separate him from all the junk
piled up on the other side—bottle glass
and tires, rusted bedsprings, tin cans.
The print already going coppery at the edges, fading.
I tell her this is exactly the photograph

I had in mind. Then step outside—the picture
gone to negative now, the street dead-ending
into saltgrass. After the news came, I kept seeing
the road in his poem disappearing—
his car stalled, the silence filling it like water,
shoring itself up against the worn stone of his voice:

I wasn't afraid, I should have been afraid.
And: *I could hear time cease, the field quietly widen.*

In the Pines

I'm going where the cold winds blow.
In the pines, in the pines, where the sun don't never shine,
I'll shiver the whole night through.

Leadbelly, "Where Did You Sleep Last Night"

1. Counterpane

The air in that last room
was a quilt weight in the cold.
I was remembering my grandmother's
upstairs bedrooms in December, brittle
plastic clouding each window,
coal dust breathing out of the pillows.

Double Wedding Ring, Joseph's Coat,
Old Maid's Puzzle. Those old quilts of hers,
four or five deep. Any hands that stitched them
gone a century or more.
How it felt to draw them over me.

2. Miss Rule

Wavered there, then, at the foot of my bed,
as much a ghost as she ever was in life.
Miss Rule, grade school substitute teacher—
Miss Ruler, we called her, skeletal and towering,
wooden twelve-inch at the ready. She looked
at least eighty even then, creped skin
and two mouths, the second lipsticked in scarlet
just west of her real one. But what terrified most
was the poem she always wielded—Eugene Field's
"Little Boy Blue." She read it in every visitation—

third-grade math, fifth-grade science—recited it
like a witness, like penance, both mouths trembling.
All our small faces struck dumb at the thought
of those dusty, rusting toys—*a boy died, a boy died*—
she'd walk in and we knew it was coming.

3. REVIVAL

My mother says I dreamed this,
my grandfather driving me in his black Buick
the summer I was ten, deep into the country.
Spit of gravel a long time, dust and the tar

that tamped it down. Then a hike
through the pines to a clearing where everyone
was singing their glory hallelujahs.
Sepia tint, the place poor as a migrant camp

and everyone dressed like the thirties.
The women with funeral smiles, their fingers
brushing my shoulders like dark sunlight.
Two fiddlers were leaning into the old hymns,

cutting them sideways, jagged, roughhewn—
you could fall a long time inside those open fifths,
you could make yourself a bed there
and never get up again. The songs

sounded like stories still happening somewhere,
like a baptismal river, everyone going under.

We shall meet on that beautiful shore.
If this was a dream, it's not gone

the way of them—those ghost-train fiddlers
leaning black against the firelight, sparks
flying up to the pine spires. *Man is born to trouble,*
my grandfather would say, and every swaying

body there knew it, in the grim grip
of their bibles—the sorrow of belief,
the low notes of faith—the "old weird
America," the sweet by and by.

4. Death in the Woods

The story is about the storyteller,
about getting the telling right.

The narrator is recalling the winter
he and his brother, just boys, found a woman

frozen to death in the woods.
She's been made old before her time

by a hard life, hard men. She's beautiful
in death, of course. Her clothes worried

from her body by a pack of dogs
that have circled her dying, left an iced zero

around her in the clearing. It's that circle
in the story that always gives me solace,

the drumbeat of that path, the dogs running
nose to tail. And the boy, now a man,

can't stop telling this story. He invents a life
for the woman in an effort toward honor,

he erases it and starts again because
to be done with it is a disservice. The point

of the story is to keep her cold mystery,
keep that circle drawn around her

higher and higher, a glass wall, keep everyone
from getting any closer.

5. SHAPE NOTE

Like the dream of the staircase that kept winding higher
        and tighter, the steps narrowing until they were doll steps;
at the top, just a landing, attic warmth of the floorboards—

the safe, still twilight a fine dust on my hands,
        small window squaring the silence.
Through it, moon and pines, the road between them receding,

the silver thread of a river.
        And I no more a stranger nor a guest.
And I no more a stranger nor a guest.

THE EYE DEMANDS A HORIZON

Sorrow roll away roll
away say the tumbleweeds

Pillar of dust
little dirt devil
spin yourself out

This is where the sun stops
settle the geese on the playa

Stay put the cattle nod
cleaving to the earth's curve
There is time enough

The wind sweeps from every direction
says *This all belongs to me*

while swallows score their sidewise
arcs and swift clouds
lift seraph wings

Whatever went before
is long gone from you now

Cures and Maxims: The poem freely adapts Old English wisdom literature as well as medical and magical prose from the *Lacnunga* and *Laecboc* and other sources, drawing upon texts in Burton Raffel's *Poems and Prose from the Old English* (Yale, 1998) and Karen Louise Jolly's *Popular Religion in Late Saxon England* (University of North Carolina Press, 1996), among others. The poem quotes from Raffel's translation of *Maxims I*, and the final line is the refrain from his translation of the Exeter Book poem, *Deor*.

Firelands: The Firelands are counties in northern Ohio which were originally part of the Connecticut Western Reserve. During the Revolutionary War, the British destroyed most of the property in this area, and the owners demanded reimbursement from the legislature. 500,000 acres were set off for them in the 1790's; the area was known first as "The Sufferers' Land," and later as the "Fire Lands." The mine fire referred to was set by striking miners in New Straitsville, Ohio, in 1884; the fire has not yet been extinguished.

Clear Mirror Lament: The italicized line is from Meng Hao-jan's "After Chang Yuan's *Clear Mirror Lament*," translated by David Hinton.

After Vermeer: The section entitled "Woman in Blue Reading a Letter" includes a variant on W.S. Merwin's well-known single-line poem, "Elegy": *Who would I tell it to.*

No Tutor But the North: Emily Dickinson to T.W. Higginson, November 1871: "If I exceed permission, please excuse the bleak simplicity that knew no tutor but the North." (*The Letters of Emily Dickinson*, vol. 2, edited by Thomas H. Johnson [Harvard University Press, 1958]). The poem is indebted to Jim Dine's monograph of heliogravures, *Birds* (Steidl, 2001); the Dine quotations are from his essay, "Reconstructing the Dream

Called 'North.'" The Tu Fu quotations are from two of the many versions of the final image in his poem "Night Thoughts": Burton Watson's translation in *The Columbia Book of Chinese Poetry: From Early Times to the Thirteenth Century* (Columbia University Press, 1984) and Red Pine's in *Poems of the Masters* (Copper Canyon Press, 2003).

The Wakeful Bird Sings Darkling: Milton, *Paradise Lost*, iii, lines 38-39.

The Woman's Lament: This is a loose adaptation and truncation of the Old English elegy sometimes entitled "The Wife's Lament."

This is a Song: The title and italicized lines are from Margaret Wise Brown's children's classic, *Little Fur Family* (Scholastic, 1946).

River: For Larry Levis.

Bright Absentee: Dickinson, J339, Fr367.

Lesson: For Charles Wright.

In the Pines: "Old weird America" is Greil Marcus's coinage, from his *Invisible Republic: Bob Dylan's Basement Tapes* (Harcourt, 1998). The poem's final line is adapted from the Isaac Watts hymn, "Resignation," itself a version of Psalm 23.

The Eye Demands a Horizon: Ralph Waldo Emerson: "The health of the eye seems to demand a horizon. We are never tired, so long as we can see far enough."

Acknowledgments

Grateful acknowledgement is made to the editors of the following publications in which these poems first appeared, sometimes in earlier versions:

The Cortland Review, Dickinson Review, FIELD, The Greensboro Review, The Iowa Review, Meridian, New Virginia Review, Poetry ("Clinic," "Chronic Town"), and *TriQuarterly.*

"After the Auction of My Grandmother's Farm," "Chequamegon," "Chronic Town," "Imaginary," "Carpathian Frontier," and "River" also appeared in *Hammer and Blaze: A Gathering of Contemporary American Poets,* edited by Ellen Bryant Voigt and Heather McHugh (University of Georgia Press, 2002).

"After Vermeer" was reprinted in *The Cambridge Companion to Vermeer,* edited by Wayne E. Frantis (Cambridge University Press, 2001).

I wish to express deep gratitude for their friendship, guidance, and encouragement to Carol Muske-Dukes, Debra Nystrom, Peter Turchi, Ellen Bryant Voigt, and Alan Williamson, and to editor Martha Rhodes and her colleagues at Four Way Books for their patience, perspicacity, and faith. Devotion *in memoriam* to Jane Cooper, Deborah Hilty, Larry Levis, Charles Modlin, and Renate Wood.

Thanks also to the National Endowment for the Arts; Hawthornden Castle in Lasswade, Scotland; the Sherwood Anderson Foundation; and St. Benedict Monastery in St. Joseph, Minnesota, for generous fellowships which made the creation of many of these poems possible.

Debra Allbery won the Agnes Lynch Starrett Prize for her first book, *Walking Distance.* Other awards include two NEA fellowships, two fellowships from the New Hampshire State Council on the Arts, the "Discovery"/ *The Nation* prize, and a Hawthornden fellowship. Her work has appeared in *FIELD, The Kenyon Review, Ploughshares, Poetry, TriQuarterly, The Yale Review,* and elsewhere. She has been writer-in-residence at Phillips Exeter Academy and Interlochen Arts Academy, and has taught at Dickinson College and the University of Michigan. Currently the director of the Warren Wilson MFA Program for Writers, she lives near Asheville, NC, with her husband and son.